meditations *for* makers

daily affirmations *for a* creative life

Deanne Fitzpatrick

NIMBUS
PUBLISHING
— NIMBUS.CA —

Nimbus Publishing Limited
3660 Strawberry Hill Street, Halifax, NS, B3K 5A9
(902) 455-4286 nimbus.ca

Printed and bound in Canada
NB1531

Editor: Emily MacKinnon
Design: Heather Bryan

Library and Archives Canada Cataloguing in Publication

Title: Meditations for makers : daily affirmations for a creative life /
     Deanne Fitzpatrick.
Other titles: Daily affirmations for a creative life
Names: Fitzpatrick, Deanne, author.
Identifiers: Canadiana (print) 20210216344
     Canadiana (ebook) 20210216379 | ISBN 9781774710029 (softcover)
     ISBN 9781774710036 (EPUB)
Subjects: LCSH: Creative ability. | LCSH: Creation (Literary, artistic, etc.) |
     LCSH: Artists—Psychology. | LCSH: Artists—Conduct of life.
Classification: LCC BF408 .F58 2021 | DDC 153.3/5—dc23

Nimbus Publishing acknowledges the financial support for its
publishing activities from the Government of Canada, the Canada
Council for the Arts, and from the Province of Nova Scotia. We are
pleased to work in partnership with the Province of Nova Scotia to
develop and promote our creative industries for the benefit of all Nova
Scotians.

for the makers.

the knitters, the rug-hookers, the weavers, the
painters, the writers, the potters, the gardeners,
the homemakers, the cooks...to all of you who turn
your hands to something.

this book is for you.

Introduction

we were made and we are makers

Whether we are cooking supper, building sandcastles, or creating fine art, we all make. We all turn our hands to something. We are all gifted. This is something I think a lot about because making is what I do every day. I try, every single day, to make my life beautiful. Sometimes I do this by writing or creating artwork, but sometimes it is just cooking supper, arranging skeins of wool in my studio, or placing a rock in the perfect spot beside a lamp on the table.

"Making" is a big and meaningful word and it matters. It matters deeply to me and to all those who spend their time creating. For me, it's a practice, and one I have worked tirelessly at.

I have a natural curmudgeonly tendency, and I have had to work at being more appreciative. (I actually remember being a young woman and driving in the car one day, complaining to my husband about the sunshine.) It has not always been easy, and learning gratitude is still challenging for me. But age has helped with that. Because over the years, I have seen what beauty does.

It enlightens people.

It strengthens people.

It deepens people.

Making things is one way to bring beauty into the world and that, in and of itself, is meaningful work. It is work worth thinking about. So that's what I've done in the following thoughts and meditations; I have reflected on my life, my relationships, my community, and my work because they are all important facets of my making.

These words are introspective reflections—the kind that float in, unbidden, when you move one hand over another. They are the small discoveries I've made in the process of making things (mostly rugs) over a period of thirty years at the frame. I am under no illusions that they are bits of deep philosophical wisdom; they are merely my own personal truths. I just thought, since we are all essentially makers, you might find some truth in them, too.

I encourage you to write in this book; use it to come to some understanding of your own truths. For we are all seeking, you and me, we are all making, and we are all here together.

There are times it is important to let things go.
It is okay to leave things unfinished. To abandon
them. What's not okay is to let those abandoned
projects keep you from starting again or interfere
with inspiration. Set them free. Unravel, unmake
them. Let them go and free your creative spirit to
be filled with something new.

It is a good day when you see the beauty in the
ordinary. It is an even better day when you see
the beauty in the broken, the left behind, the
unwanted. These are the days you have an artist's
eyes.

I like to close my eyes as I hook so I can feel the stitches instead of thinking about them.

There will never be the perfect colour.
 There will always be many good colours.
There will never be the perfect design.
 There will always be many good designs.

~ deanne fitzpatrick ~

Rugs are meant to be made, waiting to be made. Your frame and wool are there in front of you and they are calling out to you to sit with them and keep them company.

Blessed be the makers
    for they find hope
in the unknown.
    On they seek when it seems
there is nothing
    to find.

They lift the cloth to see
    what lies beneath.
Hands in motion.
    Hands make, so the soul can
rise and find its
    place, home.

Words, or something simple
    like a bowl to
hold the spirit.

I still feel a little bit off. I know the things
that will fix it: exercise, creativity. So I try to lose
myself in the things I love. I also pray. That works
for me. I am able to process my thoughts a bit (but
I try not to *over*-process them). And then...I try to
let go.

The rain continued into the morning. Still, I went
for a swim. The raindrops were hitting the water,
making little crystals bouncing on the bay. All
around me was a sea of fairy lights. I can close my
eyes now and see it again any time I want.

4   ⁓ deanne fitzpatrick ⁓

I need to make rugs. Because making feels right and it brings me back to myself, the self that believes in hope and joy and wonder and love even when there is big change. And that's the self I want to keep in touch with.

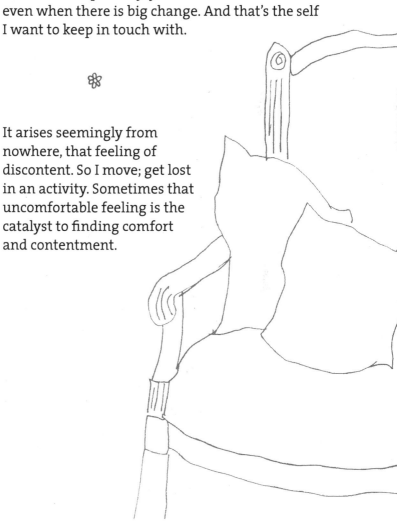

It arises seemingly from nowhere, that feeling of discontent. So I move; get lost in an activity. Sometimes that uncomfortable feeling is the catalyst to finding comfort and contentment.

Sometimes I can smell the farm
    when I lay the cream wool in the water
and watch the indigo blue
    blossom,
changing what was into what will be.
    The mud and straw on my boots.
I am there.

    I lift it out to see it new.
Blue sky. Water. Hydrangea.
    One stitch at a time,
it will become any of these.
    I take the strands in my hands
and find a new way for them
    to belong
in my time and place.

Others with a quieter mind might not need it, but
I have long accepted that, for me, the joy is in the
progress. My contentment comes from doing. As I
write and as I hook, my mind quiets. For me, this
is the only stillness I know.

deanne fitzpatrick

What is a prayer but a thank-you? Meister Eckhart said, "If the only prayer you ever say in your entire life is thank you, it will be enough."

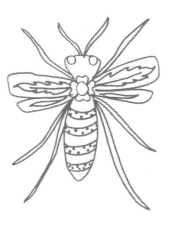

Never take memory for granted. For memory is the pathway to all you have ever loved, and all you have ever known.

All around me, doors shut.

    The world retreated.

I retreated.

    Still, I hooked my rug, for it remained the only answer.

Gosh, how I love those liturgical words, *Ordinary Time*—the days outside of Christmastide and Eastertide. I'll be walking up the steps to go in the house and the words come to my mind and I'll be reminded that right now, this ordinary time, is good enough. Better than good enough, right now is just right.

⌢ deanne fitzpatrick ⌢

When I make things, I lay everything bare. *Here is my offering*, I seem to say. *This is me; this is all I have.* I lay it before others with love, and hope for the same in return.

I wish every morning could
be like this.
    A walk.
Some tea.
    Some peace.
No fear,
    no anger.

I put the stores
    in the cupboard
before I sleep
    so I can wake up
and hear the songs
    of the day;
a chance
    to sing along.

For years I lamented leaving Newfoundland at sixteen. That loneliness, that absence of belonging...it was at the root of my art. But I came to belong again. Mostly I belong to art, rather than to a place. I finally have shelter again.

Distraction is the war of art. Sometimes I look at my phone and say to it, "You have nothing for me." It surprises me, the power in that statement. That a statement itself could change the way I feel.

⌒ deanne fitzpatrick ⌒

If we listen to our hands, they can carry us to wisdom. It does not happen quickly and it's never complete, but there is always that potential when you sit down to make.

Put your head down and do what you do. Do it as best as you can and stay focused on that. Don't worry about what someone else is making—only you can make what you make.

There are times when no words come. I fill the time with doing things. During these times I don't feel stuck—just absent. Absent from the words, the page, the story. Then one morning I come back. Reluctantly, reverently, thinking perhaps I have said all I have to say. That's when I bow my head and hope.

Don't hide the tools your hands desire. Leave them out at the ready so you can sit for five or ten minutes or two hours. Leave them there in the middle of your life to remind you what they have to offer. Set them up like an altar to your hands.

We all make things. Supper, for example. It takes effort. Perhaps for hours you are just making an aroma—one that sails through the house. Then the company opens the door and knows they are welcome.

Preparation.
Hands at work.
Love made real.

Making is as a simple as this.

I want to be known. I make so others will know me. I want to be understood, to be seen, to be noticed.
I make so I will be here.

Do you ever just love a word?
"Cultivate." I love the way my tongue
touches my teeth when I say it; it rolls
around in my mouth. I love the *feeling* I
get from the word, what it makes me see.
Then I use it a lot. "Organic." Everything begins
to seem like the word. "Relationship." Then I
use it too much and need a new word to love; a
new word to understand and explain my world.
"Thesaurus." But the search is never easy; words
have to strike a deep chord. "Meaningful." I am
searching for meaning.

Making is often humble work. Using torn bits of
cloth, a thread, a needle. Simple tools that remind
you of the power in humility.

"No" is a complete sentence. Even if something is lovely or amazing or awe-inspiring. It is okay to say no just because you want to stay home and make something small.

I want to listen more and I want to listen better. Now is a really good time for listening. Right now, in this moment.

As I hook this week I plan to listen. Listen to sounds of the birds in the morning. Listen to my husband's laugh. Listen to my heart.

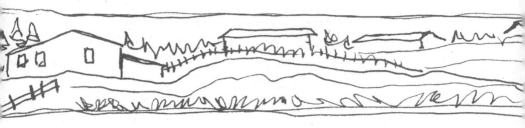

A Prayer

May my hands be good to others.
    May they hold out
hope in sorrow,
    food in hunger,
warmth in cold.
    May they make beauty
for its own sake
    without guile or cunning.

May that beauty
    rest the eyes of the lonely,
soften the hearts of the angry,
    and leave a little spirit.

I make to bring beauty into the world, and to heal
brokenness—mine and that of others. I make for
peace, for promise, for purpose.

At first, I thought Instagram was a place to go and get inspired for art. But after years of scrolling, I have learned that my inspiration comes from my life, not my phone.

My heart beats faster when I know I am making something really beautiful. There is a physical response to what is happening in my hands. Lean into it and notice the changes. The excitement of making is completely unknown unless you have made.

Find the love you need. Hold out your hand and see who takes it.
Don't let yourself be lonely—reach out.
Don't count the times someone reaches back. Just call them up and make plans. We are meant to be here for each other.

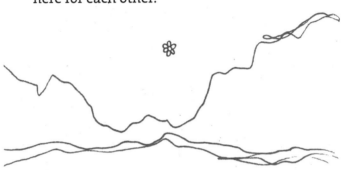

Show up. Sit up. Shut up. Do the work.
Today, that's my mantra.

～ deanne fitzpatrick ～

On my pantry shelf
    there is a jar of maple syrup.
He tapped the trees
    and boiled off the sap
and brought it for us
    in a whiskey jar.

We are all making, you know.
    Finding our way
through the forest
    so we can get back to
ourselves.

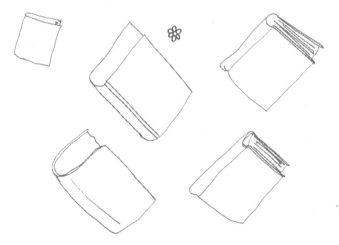

Possibilities. *What don't I know that I like?* Oh,
goodness, I love that question. It makes me so
curious. What flavours, ideas, books are out there
that I don't even know about? I know there is so
much. So much to find out.

I need a pencil and paper to let loose the worry of what I didn't do. Of what I need to do. Of tomorrow.

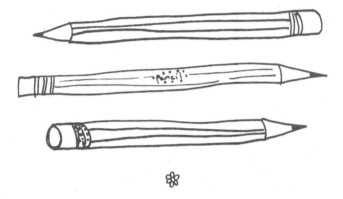

Hand over hand, mind in the moment—it is what so many are searching for, and there it is, lying beside us in a pile of rags. Transformation waiting to happen in us, and in the rags themselves. I am going to the frame now, humble and hopeful. I will see what happens and I will take what comes.

Little branches of forsythia and daffodils are the brightest bit of early spring. Willow branches. These flowers from the yard had no intention of inspiring a series. They are happy enough just to be on my kitchen table. I am the one who has intentions for them.

When I feel scared or stressed, I always turn to faith. Whether it's faith in my family and my community, faith in God, or faith in humanity. Faith, regardless of your spiritual inclination, is important. It is like a foundation; the solid structure that souls and hope and art are built upon.

In the night it is just me; I feel alone. Then I remember that the light will come again. The sun will rise and I will feel its company.

Things will be okay.

Sometimes I visit another artist's studio and seeing how they make leads me back to my own art. It always makes me want to go home and make something. And it doesn't matter if the artist is a potter or a painter—I catch the spirit they put into their work, and I want to go put it into mine.

Three days, three rugs. I am on fire! I feel so happy and inspired because I made three rugs. Only one of which I really love. Two are fine. The one rug that feels nearly perfect (it isn't) shows you that if you rage on, good things will happen. Not everything will be good, but good things will happen.

I never think about how long it takes to make something. Instead, I think about how much quiet time I'll have with myself as I do.

Open. Open to new thoughts, new ideas, new ways of seeing, of being. I have to stay open. Wide open, arms out, ready to take hold. Ready to let go.

But, at the same time, I need ritual and habit. That is the only way I can make art.

They don't like each other, these two things. They want different things altogether.

Happily, the spirit of art can be divided. It loves them both.

In my experience, ideas get better when you play with them. They take you down a path, following clues and discovering possibilities. I love when a new idea comes to me because I'm never certain where it will lead me.

Whatever kind of life we have, as long as it is built around peace, commitment, and loving care, it is completely normal. Normal is defined inside of peoples' lives and not by touched-up pages or social media feeds.

I do what I can so I don't go into that place where just *being* scares the shit out of me. I read, study, plan. I call my friends. I teach myself new things. I make. I cook. Work is my tonic; it bridges the gap between the places my imagination *could* go, and the beauty of existing moment to moment, day to day.

As makers, we often need time to ourselves. But when we lift our heads, many of us find that we need connection as well. I think we can be both introverted and extroverted, needing different things at different times, even on the same day.

This pear I found when I was buying apples at the market; it was worth the trip to just find this exquisitely shaped piece of fruit.

These are the little things that inspire us. Be on the lookout for them. They are important. Even on a Saturday morning drive to a small city in the middle of winter, you can find a little piece of August.

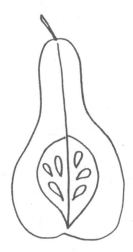

deanne fitzpatrick

The goal is not to always find things to hook. It is enough to find something beautiful. Something you can put on your table and look at every time you walk in the room. Then you see that beauty is bountiful. In a rock, a cracked shell, a shard of pottery. There is so much beauty in what we find on the ground beneath our feet.

A Prayer

A night sky so big
    and a fire flickering
long lines of spark
    words written in the dark blue

remember that night
    when the peepers sang glory be
and we sat in
    parkas and were glad

to have each other
    if not to hold
at least to love.

In cleaning the studio I sometimes find bits of
cloth and yarn that belong to a different time and
place. A colour I used to love, or old grey trousers
I once thought would make great cliffs. But now I
say goodbye; there's no hanging on, no saving for
later. Open the windows so new winds can blow
through.

You have to follow the part of you that is quiet
on the inside. This silent longing in us requires
attention, even in the midst of our schedules and
plans. This is not easy for me. I have my routines
and rituals that I love, and it always feels like a
sacrifice to leave them.

⌒ deanne fitzpatrick ⌒

Notice the small changes in your work—the little things you get better at. New colours that appear, the way the pencil moves in your hand. These small things add up. Month after month, year after year, they transform your work. Sometimes you cannot see it but as long as you are making, it is happening.

Sunday morning, hard rain like a Kris Kristofferson song, and my burlap is waiting for me to create some little bit of magic. Some tiny song of joy or a moment of repose...or maybe just a mat. There is nothing wrong with just a mat. The reason we make is to make. We make so that the sound of the rain is a comfort rather than a simple downpour.

Sometimes people tell me that they stopped making because their rugs or quilts or knitted things just piled up. It always makes me sad for what they've lost, for what they've given up. I just hope they find their way back to handwork. I know they often do because without it they find an absence, and it must be filled.

When my father died I hooked him with a cigarette in his hand, standing in front of the baby-blue Volkswagen. I was in the passenger seat, watching and waiting. That is what we do for each other in life—we watch and we wait. Tears fell into that rug as I hooked it, and the wool absorbed them.

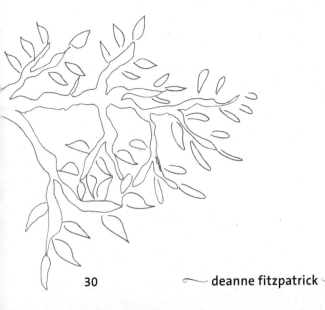

deanne fitzpatrick

Just get up and get at it. Don't think too long. Don't commiserate with yourself—for God's sake don't do that. Just think how hard that must be for God to listen to. Just show up and get on with it.

My friend Rachel was considering her mugs, wondering if she was an artist or a potter. "I think," she said, "that we have a good life because people hold these pots in their hands and they make them feel good and they think of us, and good things come to us."

She said that, and still she wonders if she is an artist.

Watch what you say and what you offer. I don't mean be *stingy*—be generous with yourself and with your time—just make sure you say yes to the things that feel like yes. Say yes to the things that bring a smile to your face.

Sometimes all I hear in the studio is the birds singing. Other times I find myself alone with thoughts that go round and round until I turn on a podcast to carry me away. While making, I have learned to listen well. Both to myself and the birds.

Stop complaining. Knit instead. Hook instead.
Make something. Channel that angst into
something productive. Take it and turn it into
something beautiful. That bit of loneliness, that
bitchy feeling? It can be turned on its head and
into something else...just by moving your hands
in the right direction.

I can feel when I need to make space between
myself and something else. Sometimes it is
some*one* else. It is not that there is something
wrong, really. There is just a feeling that
something is not quite right, but I can't pinpoint
it. Kahlil Gibran said we need space in our
togetherness and he was right.

I like to look into the woods by the side of the road as I walk. The undergrowth, the ferns. They are so beautiful even in the shadows. You do not have to be in the full shine to glow. You can glow in your own little space, the one you carved out for yourself.

The people who choose to hook rugs have made a statement about life. They have said: "I am going to slow down while the world is speeding up."

I don't think, "Do I want to hook?" It is not a question I consider. I just go hook automatically. Whether I want to or not is irrelevant. I just make because it is there to be made.

For most of us, thoughts are just thoughts. They don't have control over you. You, in fact, have control over them. But it isn't easy: thoughts are demanding, spoiled, and attention-seeking. They are still just thoughts. They come and go like water flowing. You can try to sequester them, even if you can't quite tame them. You can tell them what they can and cannot do. Take them for what they are—just thoughts.

I feel grateful that after thirty years of making sometimes my hands get tired before I do. Tonight the sun went down on me and my hands got tired, but my spirit wanted to finish the rug. I always let my hands win. They have been so kind to me.

❁

My identity is lost in a million stitches. Somewhere in those stitches is my beginning and my middle. I still have time to stitch my end. In all that handwork is my love, my losses, my frustration, my joy, my loneliness, my yearning—my story. Out there somewhere in a million stitches.

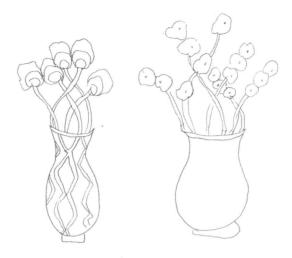

Sometimes I feel guilty drinking out of a pretty mug because a potter did not make it. Because I am more alone with my coffee than I would be with a handmade mug.

I learned faith, I chose faith. I use it in my work, I use it in my life. I carry it with me, cupped in my hands. But I have to keep my hands together to hang onto it—and this takes some attention. And sometimes when I am with someone who needs a little, I open my hands and let it spill over.

Don't rush the last few hours, the last few minutes, of making something. Sometimes I do, and I end up missing the chance to give it that extra flourish, those special details that deepen it. The end of a project is a time to make it a bit better. It is a time to be present, to savour, to enrich. Don't rush it. Love it.

It isn't until halfway through that a creative project starts to look like maybe it isn't working out. It is so common to have a time when the work looks like it should be left behind. Remind yourself that now is the time to press on. You can really only know if it's no good once it's done.

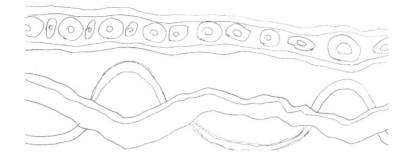

These little lives we have are sacred and we should hold them in our hands like a robin's nest holding eggs. We are just as fragile. We need tending and care. We need to be held safely, loved deeply.

Getting flustered eats up my creative energy. It is like a creative act, all that chasing yourself around and being out of sorts. It takes up good energy and leaves you zapped and feeling wasted. So save it. Save it for the making.

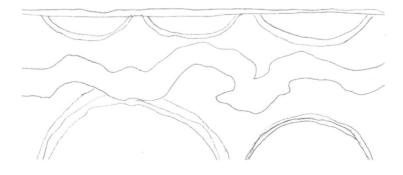

I could be better.
    I could give more away
I could never speak ill
    of another.
Harder still,
    I could never think ill of another.
I could be better.
    I could always be better.

Wherever you are and whatever you learn or become, where you come from never changes. It is the root of who you are, and the root of what you make.

~ deanne fitzpatrick ~

It takes a mile or two of walking to get to my frame. To show up in the right place, in the right space. That half an hour of going nowhere seems to always take me somewhere. My neighbour asks how I can walk down the same road day after day. I tell him it is never the same way twice.

I like the idea that wool began in a field, that it is natural. I step away from acrylics and polyester because to me they have no life in them; they're from a factory. Wool adds life to my rugs.

Feeling free to make anything without evaluation is the beginning of real beauty.

Spend some time on yourself. Spend it like it's pocket money and you are a child. Spend it on your creativity. You need to buy time to make. You buy it from yourself.

"Create beauty every day" is a powerful commitment. It changes how I see things, how I do things. The way I spend my time. It makes me look at my hands differently: as the way out, or the way through.

We make to connect. So someone will feel our love in the socks on their feet, taste our love in that loaf of bread dropped off just when we needed it most. I write to reach out. I write to let you know that I am here and that I am no different than you. I write so that I can be.

If you do not know what you are going to make tomorrow, look to your past. Pull out old sketchbooks. Write down old stories. Remember what you knew when you were young.

Each time you begin again you will have to find a new way because living gets in the way and you'll see it differently than you used to.

I still get up in the morning and say, "Rejoice, this is the day the Lord has made." Yup, I actually say that. And yup, it helps. I know it doesn't help everyone but it helps me. For it is a day. And grey though it may be, it can still be filled with whatever beauty I can muster.

Being an artist is just a job. You make stuff out of other stuff. You make it a bit different each time. "Artist." It's just a word. A word I was so unfamiliar with it took me years to admit that that I was one.

Walks in the woods through bramble and thicket.
　　Trails lost and overgrown,
reassured once in a while by
　　hunter-orange ribbon.
Cold, wet Sunday in the winter.
　　I want to be here.
But mostly I want to be home
　　with papers and bits of wool.
Yet, if I am not here
in this white wonderland
　　I won't feel the goodness
　　of being home by the wood stove
in the same way.
　　Nor will I see what that fabric can become.
Space from the studio.
　　Wide open spaces to be lived in
so art has a reason
　　and I have a reason to make it.

The other day I was helping a woman draw a
pattern on a backing. I cut out some paper shapes
and she laid them down so nicely on the linen.
For a second, I wanted her to take all the perfect,
laid-out-just-right pieces and throw them around.
Instead, I smiled and lifted one and moved it
aside, then took another and laid it on top. I drew
her a line. She reached for the pen.
   Then I knew I could teach.
Then she knew she could draw.
   Then we smiled together.

Whenever I sit with my sketchbook, the sudden
emptiness of a blank page seems too good for a
scribble; too precious to waste. I grew up drawing
on the end pages of the novels my father read.

Sometimes people wonder whether they should use linen or burlap for their rugs. "Which lasts longer?" they ask. And in their sincerity, they forget how quickly a mug shatters on a marble counter, yet the potter still makes the mugs. They will last as long as they last. What will it matter in the end?

Wake up.
Forget the email—it will be there
later. Sit with your hands and
make the thing that makes
you.
Love it a bit before you
give in to the calls of
the day.

Colour evokes feeling. My studio is packed with vibrancy. I love it, I want it. I would not have it any other way. But when I go home, I want everything soothing and soft. I want calm.

Use the best materials that you can get your hands on when you are making something. You are worth it, your hands are worth it, the work is worth it.

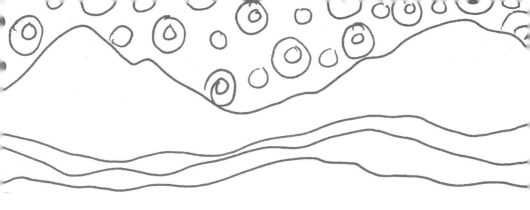

An artist once told me that she never hoards
her ideas for later because the more she uses
them up, the more ideas come to her. So use it
up. Whatever you've got, just use it up and make
room for what will come.

That snow that is falling ever so gently is an
invitation
    to sit at the frame
to be home bound.
    to be grateful for slippery roads
and winter sleeps.
    It is an invitation to read
the book,
    to bake the big chicken.
Snow brings a silence
    to savour.
A gentle reminder that we are here
    just to be.
We are here to witness it falling upon our mitt.

I am not one who says things don't matter. I grew up with little. One pair of shoes, one jacket, that sort of thing. I enjoy the beauty of abundance by times. But the thing that matters to me more is remembering that I have a lot. That is when I am happiest.

Sit with the joy of making. Hold still with it. You can feel it in your hands, but mostly you can feel it in your heart.

deanne fitzpatrick

Sometimes, if I want to celebrate, I buy some fingernail polish. When I get home, I clean and file my nails and rub them with rose- or almond-scented oil. I treat them like they are beautiful, these old hands of my mother's. I smile at them and thank them. It's a small celebration, just between me and my hands.

Have you ever been embarrassed by someone you love? Can we hold those two feelings—affection and embarrassment—together?

Then I remember: to love another is to let them be themselves. And so I love them, even as they are...and hope they will love me, even as I am.

No one looks forward to a rainy day like a maker does. There is no call to go outside and enjoy the day. You are free to sit at home and make the quilt, knit the sweater, or hook the rug. Rainy days were meant for us.

People sometimes tell me that after they learned to hook rugs, they never saw the world the same way again. Suddenly they saw the greens in the grass and the blues in the sky in ways they never had. Making did not just open their hands, it opened their eyes.

Next thing they know, it opens their hearts.

Barnacles. I can still see them on the enormous black rocks of the beach below my childhood home. I was always drawn to nature and form, and creams and whites.

We must look closely in order to recreate. We must know something intimately if we want to explore it. If we want to turn it inside out. Often, it is just a matter of remembering.

Handwork is a gift. Not the thing you make, but the making of it.

There is ease in being together.
    Joy found in the pure moments
of walking down a rural road
    where leftover farms
have found new homes
    in the bramble.

There is good love
    found in wanting your friends
to float on small waves of success,
    knowing that when we come through
our front doors, it is only what happens there
    that matters at all.

Knowing that someone sees your heart
    and believes in your goodness
is reason enough to be alive.
    no need to search too hard when you have
friends that remember you.

We are sensitive souls. We know that loving to
make things is the business of beauty. It is the
domain of the softer, kinder ones. We are a gang
of our own. We care where things come from,
who loved them, who brought them into being.
We are the makers.

⁓ deanne fitzpatrick ⁓

Quiet the podcasts, or the noise you use to free yourself. Because it is not freeing you—it is filling your head with thoughts and ideas that only add to the clutter. Turn everything off. Turn down the noise and you'll finally feel that you have the right to speak.

When I was a child I had no idea what good company my hands would be. How they would bless my days. How they would stave off insecurity and loneliness. Back then, I took them for granted.

I love my phone way too much. It nags at me to pick it up. It keeps my mind racing, thinking, looking, instead of relaxing, wandering, loosening. Maybe if I start thinking of it as something that gets in the way of my creativity I could change the way I feel about it. Let's reframe it. Let's leave it behind. Let's put it down.

Colour talks, if only you'd listen. When you lay one out it calls to another. Yellow says, "Bring me blue." Red cries out for coral to join it. We just have to stay quiet and listen.

There is no "alone" when I am at the studio. As I go through my cloth I see my husband's old blue sweater, the last bits of my mother's green wool coat (she died twenty years ago). The little silk scarf my father-in-law tucked into his suit jacket. The satin lining of my twelve-year-old son's brown cloth coat (he's twenty-eight now).

You'd think it would be lonely, but it isn't.

Sometimes when I read a poem or a novel, I see a rug. It comes as no surprise to me that words paint pictures and inspiration is everywhere.

I once knit a black cashmere turtleneck sweater full of dropped stitches and other teeny-tiny flaws. I gave it to my friend Nancy who likes everything just so. She likes it because now I am with her on cold, damp days, flaws and all.

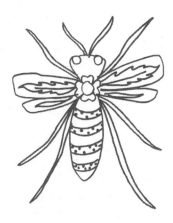

Being awake in the middle of the night for any length of time leads me to wonder about the immensity of it all. At the same time, I worry about the minutiae. The dark likes to challenge my faith. But I wait until the morning, and there my faith is again.

Know that when you make, you are powerful. You transform. You take one thing and make another.

I wonder if my grandmothers, in their rural houses with outdoor plumbing, ever needed to remind themselves to be in the moment. Making porridge, gutting fish, carrying water, hooking rugs, tending a garden...these are all things that keep us attached to time while still being able to get lost in the moment. A special kind of mindfulness.

Making something is an act of faith. You are not quite sure it will all work out, but you stay at it and act as if it will.

Thinking about the rug
    lonely on the frame
in the studio.
    My affection for it
is just beginning.
    It is new friendship.
Sometimes I am not sure.
    How much do I say?
How long should I stay?
    What should I bring you
so you'll know
    that my intentions
are good?

～ deanne fitzpatrick ～

Walking is a prelude to making. It is the warm-up. It can also be the in-between time. That space in the day to find a new path through the piece you are working on. It is as much a part of the process as cutting up the wool.

I sometimes only find the story in a rug long after I have made it. A sudden realization of what was happening in my unconscious as I hooked. It's then that I know there are things going on in my mind below the surface, and rug-hooking finds them.

I find it interesting how alone I feel with my thoughts sometimes, but as soon as I share them I discover that others are feeling the exact same thing. This has happened over and over. It is a consistent pattern for me: retreating and then reaching out.

Sewing might be about healing wounds. Big gaping holes patched over, sewn together with tiny tender stitches. Never quite the same as it was, different now than before, but still with plenty of life left in it.

Some days I know that blue belongs with me and red has to be banished. Other days I belong to red and blue does not get a mention. It starts in the morning I suppose, or perhaps while I'm asleep. Things go on in me that I have no idea about and the only sign I get is the colour my hands are reaching for.

It seems many of us have a favourite tree. Often it is stoic, alone in a field. Perhaps in it we see ourselves.

You can't knit peace into a family or a community by making a sweater. But you can knit peace within yourself by making it, and that's a start.

Do you ever wonder if you are making art or craft? It doesn't matter. Just make. It is the making that matters.

Don't be afraid to call yourself an
artist. An artist is just someone who
thinks up stuff and makes it.
That's all.

My friend Brenda transformed her nice big
bedroom into her studio. Her bed was relegated to
the old studio, a small guest room. She explained,
"I only sleep in the bedroom; I live my life in my
studio."

Youthfulness is part of creativity; it is constant renewal. So hang on to your swagger, because you'll need it to keep bringing beauty into the world.

Every bloom must hope to enchant an artist.

When I look at those simple lines of a tree or a chair or a flower I am sure I can draw it. Then I sit down and learn that even the simplest of lines have their secrets. What I draw is something different than what I saw.

But I begin to see that, although I might not think it is as good, my drawing, too, has its secrets.

Beauty is everywhere. You can find it at your feet, in the sky above you, in the dead plants on the side of the road in winter. All you have to do is decide that it is there, and you'll see it.

I made my daughter a quilt. Just a big floppy thing, nothing fancy. After university she brought it home and it sits in the closet. I realize that I made it as much for myself as for her, to reconcile her leaving and time passing. But I will leave it in the closet because I know one day she'll see it and understand.

Resistance is always there. In order to make, you need to stand up against it and go forward and bring the thing to life even if other people might think you are foolish for doing so.

So much of being a maker is curating yourself. But if you are too selective, too picky, nothing rises to the top—ideas go on forever and nothing gets made. But if you are not picky enough, well, that's not good either. What is important is that you make.

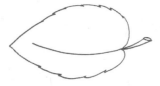

deanne fitzpatrick

The thing I love about spring is that the evenings are long and are just right for making. The new evening light means I can see my colours as they are and keep making until I meet the night.

Kitchen flowers picked from our garden, or perhaps just a tree branch in water ready to bloom. Grocery store tulips doing somersaults on your table. All of these remind you of the beauty beyond your four walls, and lure you to feel the ground under your feet.

Colours are infinite, and there will always be new ways of marrying them together.

On the table: two green pears and a golden beeswax candle. I am happy to have taken a moment to really look at those pears. A moment is a moment, and this moment is as worthy as any other.

Boredom is your friend. Not knowing what to do with yourself will lead you places you never knew you could go. Savour it instead of filling it up.

It can be hard to admit to believing, to saying out loud that you are a woman with faith. God, it seems, has gone out of fashion these days. Still, I believe.

Make the thing you want to have. The wanting will inspire and motivate you. Don't make the thing that seems easier or the thing that will take less time. Make the thing that you want to live with, that you want to wear, that you want to love.

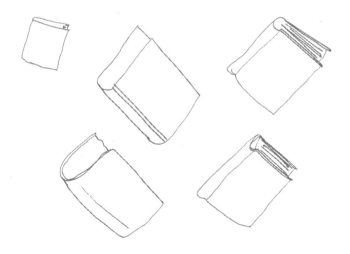

I like to take my ideas and mix them together in ways that might not necessarily make sense. It makes me happy to bring them together, have them meet each other. It's like a little party with friends of friends who may have heard about each other but have never had the chance to meet.

I started writing down how I spend my time every day. In my pencil scratches I see another day pass and I ask myself, "What did you make today?"

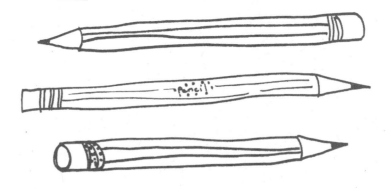

Our hands hold the secrets of our being. We are offered the chance to work out the secrets as we make.

Sometimes I write to an artist I admire—just a note to let them know I see their work. I may never hear anything back and that's okay. I just want them to know I saw it.

One of the best places I find inspiration is at my feet as I walk. Whether it is on a slushy road in winter or along the forest floor in spring, I have seen the best abstract designs on the ground in front of me.

I asked Marie Helene Allain, a nun who is also a sculptor, if she still gets down on her knees to pray and she told me: "When I work, I pray."

Don't let yourself get too stiff. Be sure to turn on the music and dance in the kitchen on a Friday night or a Tuesday afternoon or whenever you can.

We make to be seen, to be heard, to be felt, to be understood.
    We make to mend, to heal, to love.
We make to belong.
    We make to be alone with ourselves.
We make to understand.

There are times when I feel I have hooked
everything there is to hook. So I start where I
began and hook that again, and when I do it looks
so different than it did thirty years ago and I
know that there is no end in sight.

I mark the passage of summer by the ripeness
of berries. With the first flood of sunshine, we
are overloaded with strawberries. Once summer
has settled in we get the tender raspberries.
Blueberries mark August, telling us that though
the fruit is sweet, summer will soon pass and the
fields will redden again.

Jealousy is real and raw. There are so many other lives paraded before us to compare our own humdrum life to. But we forget that most of us create the life we want. We just have to get back to finding the beauty in our own lives and remember why we made the choices we did.

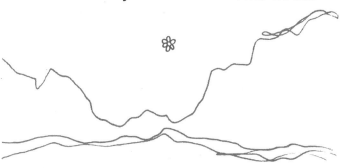

I started a gratitude journal. I hated the idea but everyone kept talking about them. I discovered that everyone is talking about them because they work.

I can hear someone hammering. They are making, too. I can listen to the music they make as I sit here and make mine. We are together.

I have been thinking for a week about a single spruce. That one-in-a-million spruce that is somehow different than all the others. On long drives along the highway it sometimes feels as if there is nothing to see—but there is always a bit of beauty begging you to find it.

⌒ deanne fitzpatrick ⌒

Little words, big words; you string them together, dreaming of meaning. Why include words in a rug unless they are worthy of making someone think?

Don't try to make art that sells; try to make art that people didn't even know they wanted, but can't forget now that they've seen it. Make art that lingers in peoples' minds and makes them catch their breath when they see it.

I paint—sometimes poorly, sometimes well.
When it is bad I just paint over it. Sometimes
when it is good I paint over it. When I paint I am a
painter.

I write because I want to talk—not because I
am a writer, but because I have something to say.
When I write I am a writer.

It is a prayer for the mountains
    that I'll never climb,
the places I'll never go.

It is a prayer for the insects
    that burrow beneath me,
the ones I'll never see.

They are there
    while I am here
in this tiny room
    making things.

And though it is sometimes hard to feel,
    they matter too, as much as me.

deanne fitzpatrick

Sometimes when I am worrying about someone, I close my eyes and picture them wrapped in a big quilt. I try to feel the warmth the quilt is offering them. I do this on my walks. It is a kind of prayer for the people I love.

People love to say, "It's beautiful." But what's really beautiful is when they can tell you *why* what you have made is beautiful, how it makes them feel, and where it brought them within themselves.

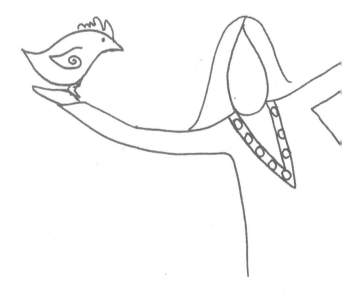

I hook because I belong to it and it belongs to me; it is something so much a part of me that I carry it with me no matter what I am doing.

Most of the time I like to do the same things day after day: walk, eat, read, hook, write, watch a show, take a bath, go to bed, get up, and do the same things again. As I tell you this it all seems so dull. Mostly, though, it makes me feel content, safe, and comfortable. I feel the stillness of it and I close my eyes
and say a prayer of
thanks
that nothing
much is
happening.

As a child I picked raspberries on that hill behind
my house. I could not believe those berries were
free and wild, buried in the field beyond the
spruce. I overcame my fears and went to gather
them. I did it quickly and I was scared, but I never
missed a season of those berries.

Paradise, my father's home
    in the middle of the bay.
I visited at fifteen,
    ate cod tongues
in a teal flat-roof house
    and brought my father
a piece of the shattered altar
    from his childhood church.
I found it years later
    in his bottom drawer
where all important things were kept.

Knowing our own goodness and calling out the
goodness in others is what loving is about. Loving
our community. Loving ourselves. Trust me, this
is not something I am only telling you; I am also
telling myself.

I think every day should be like the one where
you picked the first tomatoes of summer. We
want as many of them as we can get, yet if
we have too many, they no longer hold their
glory.

We only need to see the last of summer's
tomatoes in a bowl to really understand this.
They sit there. Too many tomatoes. What once
was precious is no longer.

How to be an artist? It's a question I think about a lot. Do I need to wear a lot of black? Do I need to take simple things and complicate them?

How about I show up day after day, alone with my ideas, and just make stuff. Anything. Just make. Is that how to be an artist?

This is a prayer for the sons and mothers
    who can't see eye-to-eye right now
and who bear the grief and feel the loss
    of the comfort they could once
give each other.
A prayer for hope to fall like a feather
    and land in the palms of their hands.

I make most of my rugs in the small studio room
in the eaves of my old house. There is plenty
of light; it is painting this page as I write. That
amber glow holds my hands, and draws me
towards the studio every morning. The light
speaks to me, invites me home.

My friend was heartbroken and the
only thing I knew to do was give her
an empty book and tell her to write.
Because she is a writer.

Nostalgia is a scary thing for me; a single sweeping moment that washes over me like a wave. The idea that times were simpler, that life was better, and before I know it I'm on the verge of sadness.

I remind myself that some day I will be nostalgic about this moment, this time, this place. Nostalgia is only good if it is fleeting.

❀

Sometimes I write or draw things on my canvas then hook right over it. No one will ever know they are there but me. Another layer of meaning in the making.

Fools abound,
    and I am glad they do.
People who love unabashedly and quickly.
    Let me be one of them.
A fool to worry.
    A fool to care.
A fool to trust.
    Let me take a chance.
A chance on someone
    who needs it.

In the morning, I take a dose of stillness. I keep
my Bible on my table, along with books of poetry
and prose. I read a few pages of them all, quietly,
while the light of the morning prepares my
studio for the day.

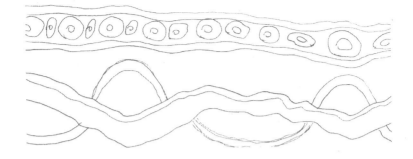

There is much beauty in imperfection. Whether it is in ourselves, our personalities, our bodies, or in the things we make. Every single thing is flawed, if that is what we are looking for. If we look for the flaw we can find it in a rose.

A house is a container for a life. It is not only an object, or a building on a piece of land. It is a place of belonging. A place we make our own. We need to nurture it so it can nurture us.

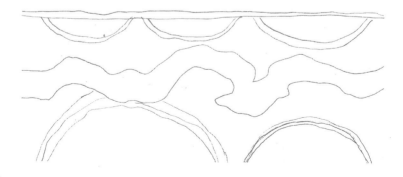

I am not afraid to draw, even badly. I do it because the doing means something—more, even, than the finished thing.

❀

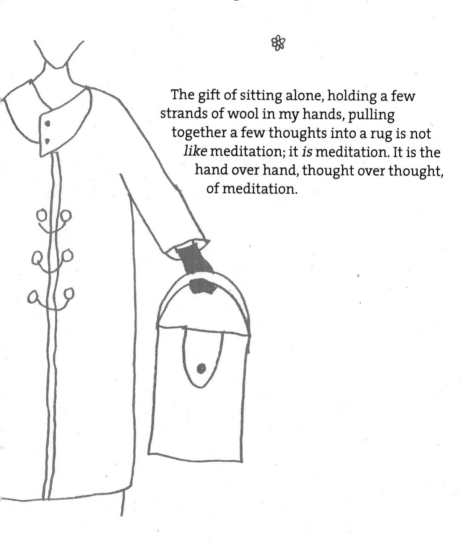

The gift of sitting alone, holding a few strands of wool in my hands, pulling together a few thoughts into a rug is not *like* meditation; it *is* meditation. It is the hand over hand, thought over thought, of meditation.

⌒ deanne fitzpatrick ⌒

Big goals are made up of tiny action after tiny action. Right now I am ready to add some things to my list. One of them is *vacuum*.

Upon reflection, I have to say that some things seem as if they don't really contribute much to the bigger goals. But these little things matter.

Help me remember this when I have to put on my parka and boots to buy milk and bread.

Prayer

For the snow that adds light to the night
for the moon that shines down upon it
for me, the little one who wanders down below it
with more questions than answers
more joy than sorrow
more love than anger.

May the moonlight lead me
to find a way to share the abundance
that has been laid bare before me
may I be good, be kind, be true,
may I love the day before me and
truly see it for the gift it is.

Amen.

For years I felt I had enough art because my walls were full. And then one day I thought, "Am I going to see the same art for the rest of my life?" Is there not room to change it up?

So I began putting away or giving away some pieces that no longer spoke to me. I want my home to make me feel. She is my muse, so I treat her with love and respect. I buy her nice things. I keep her tidy. I just love her, because that is what she needs to keep inspiring me.

I'll never finish hooking the Bay of Fundy, or Placentia Bay, or the Narrows of St. John's Harbour, because I will never ever get them right. As long as I am making, it will never be over.

Patience is mine to master. I will never really master it, but I'll never give up on it either.

These are the days to make, to create beauty for no good reason. These are the days to bake a pie. I once read you cannot be unhappy as you make a pie. I know that's not totally true, but I know a pie is bound to make someone happy.

Rugs are meant to be made. Your frame and wool are there in front of you and they are calling out to you to sit with them and keep them company. They are waiting.

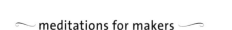

I am not always conscious of why I make every rug. Sometimes they just come out of me and I find them. It is not always deliberate, mentioned, or planned. I just start pulling loops.

I try to find answers while I make, but they are elusive. I think I find one and then time slips by and I am left wondering again. Still, I will always turn to my hands for the answers.

How are you adding beauty to the world? Once you start thinking about it you will find that there are many ways. Start being aware of it— think about it, be deliberate about it. There is no such thing as too much beauty.

Lighting the fire is a ritual. First you layer the paper, some birchbark, then kindling, and then the logs. Light the paper, open the damper, and blow a little on the fire. It is a winter rite of passage here in this old house. The fire draws us together. It is a hub of the home that needs nurturing and tending and that is why I love it.

I look at an orchid and I want to paint it in wool, even though it is more beautiful on its own than it will ever be as a painting or as a rug. And yet, I want to capture it in a way it knows nothing about—in a way that is my own.

When I was only sixteen I left Newfoundland and moved to Nova Scotia. I lost my sense of belonging for quite a while. Untethered. Forty years later, I have developed a deep sense of belonging, both here and there. I also belong in my studio, at my rug-hooking frame, to my books and papers and wool.

Walking and hooking go together so well. I always find that on my walk new ideas come to me. They pop up in unexpected places. The best way for me to get them is to not look for them; to forget about wanting a new idea at all. I go off and do something completely unrelated and new ideas emerge.

Savour the finish, the end of whatever you are making. Don't plow through it late at night to get it done. Done is not the answer. Making is the answer.

Sometimes when I write or record a podcast I worry that what I said might be misinterpreted, or someone will not like it. Then I remember: that is the risk of art. That to speak up or put yourself out there in any way is a risk that you have to take.

Love waits.
    It takes its time.
it never counts minutes or days or hours.
    It's ready for you
when you arrive
    with your hands
ready to work
    ready to make
full of hope
    and cupped with ideas.
Love makes time goes by
    —lost time
but not time lost—
    because there was that place
where you were quietly
    with yourself
just making.

Focusing on perfection in art is a barrier to
making. Things sometimes go unfinished because
expectations are so high they are unattainable. If
there is any kind of perfection in art, we know it
when we see beauty.

There are things I can only hope and wish and pray for. The big things: that my family will be healthy, that my children will thrive, that the world will be okay in this golden moment of now.

I sometimes dream of myself as a young woman, trying to decide what to do with my life. I am always a bit lost, wondering where to live or what to do. The dream always ends with me remembering I have a studio and that I make rugs. I find myself and the dream is done.

I do not have a bucket list. There is just the list of the day to day. There may never be a later. So it goes on the list for today.

I can get on people's nerves. I know that. I am single-minded; I plow ahead. When I get an idea on my mind the only way to get it off my mind is to get it done. I blunder; I make mistakes. As I get older I want to bother others less. It is that simple. So I try harder to be better and mostly I do better. Still, I don't do perfect.

Will I get an idea while I am plumping up my window boxes this afternoon? Or when I'm cutting back those old mums the frost has shattered? Who knows. You can't go into an activity expectant; that destroys the possibilities. You just have to lose yourself and see what comes.

Find the thing that is easy for you and do that. Do that over and over again. Do it with love. Do it with intention. Don't worry; this is just a starting place. Worry about getting better and better at it. That is where real beauty lies in wait.

⌐ deanne fitzpatrick ⌐

I feel the winter coming
long before the apples are shaken from their
        trees.
I am thinking of frigid things,
        of falling on ice.
Yet I look outside and
        the sun is high
and the water is still warm enough
        to swim in
and here I am
        thinking of snow
falling heavy
        on a lawn so full
of dandelions
        that the promise of winter
feels like a lie.

*And the hatches are battened with the limited
knowledge of the hearts.* I wrote this in a rug,
thinking about it the whole time I was making it.
For that is what making does for me—it helps me
process my thoughts and ideas, and it brings me
to knowledge of myself.

Born on my mother's forty-third birthday, the youngest of seven children, I was raised like an only child. Having raised six already, my mother just let me be. That freedom gave me room to think and to make and to be.

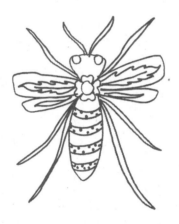

Curiosity is curly and circuitous. Following it feels like you are going nowhere. It is organic and lets one bit of knowledge build upon another, like a vine producing fruit.

"There is nothing more beautiful than an idea."
I have carried this thought around with me for
thirty years. Isn't everything an idea in some
way? The beauty in an idea is in its potential, in
its freedom and possibility to become more. An
idea has the ability to bloom.

I make lists. Lists for little things I need to pick up,
designs I might like to make, books I hear about.
Lists are like little maps. Reminders of what I
need to do to get to another place. I have never
had a lot of clarity about where I am going in life,
art, or business. I just follow these little maps and
make new ones and then I follow them wherever
they take me.

As women, do we become more powerful in our invisibility when we age? Does our influence quietly grow? A rug-hooker told me so. I'll ponder this over quite a few rugs. That's what I do. As I hook, I try to work out the questions.

There is a picture of me leaning against my father. It feels like a mirage. This man who had grade ten. He loved books. He always wanted to write a book. I write for him. I write for what he made possible for me.

Essentially, I struggle with the notion of deserving what I have. It runs deep, this imposter syndrome, and though I think about it as I hook, I have very few answers other than perhaps there is no deserving. I am just lucky. I get to make a life out of making rugs.

I love the path...down the winding road of my imagination, ferns brushing my legs and blue creeping jenny under bare feet. Sleeping under the stars of ideas, midnight in the garden of wonder. My heart feels so light when I have a new idea.

Years ago, my friend Catherine Thurston was doing the dishes in my kitchen. I can still see her holding up an old plate and telling me about the Buddhist notion of mindfulness—of how even drying a dish can be a prayer.

I made a rug with a blue field in it only to find out when the rug was finished it was a river. Often, I am making one thing and another emerges. The story of a rug is told when it is done.

I see houses on cliffs when I am half awake.
I think of those dreams as a place to go, my
imagination being fluid and free. It's a place full
of colour and possibility. I just close my eyes,
breathe slowly, and wait. You can go there
too. Just rest quietly and wait.

❀

Last week I tried to make a
painting that featured waves.
It remains incredibly bad. But
making the bad painting
may lead me to a good
rug. It is good to do
something badly. It
is humbling, and we
all need that.

When I read a novel, wishing I could write like that, it takes my focus off the beauty of the written work before me. It distracts me from focusing on getting better at and valuing what I make. Love your own work.

❀

I learned from my mother what true friendship is. It took years for it all to sink in, but it came.

You don't gossip about your
    friends, I learned.
You tell them the truth, with kind
    intentions.
You hold back the truth when
    necessary.
You sit with them when they need
    you.
You make them a cup of tea.

We practice these ancient things like weaving, knitting, and rug making. And yet it is the newest technology that has brought us together in it, and given these ancient things resurgence.

Makers work alone. We are isolated. But there are times I need to talk or to listen to a story similar to my own. I need other artists—people who understand that for us, the process is the product.

When I walk, I feel the looseness in my mind and in my stride at about one kilometre. Walking is a form of meditation. Hooking is another. Thoughts come and go. There is not one way to meditate. There is not one way to pray. There are many ways to find yourself.

 Accept love, and grace, and good fortune gratefully, and be thankful. There is no point feeling guilty for your good fortune when you could just share it.

I have read Wallace Stegner's *Crossing to Safety* many times over thirty years, and I have learned a lot about the nature of time. I have learned about the healing of old wounds. I have learned about the importance of forgiveness. I have become gentler. All of this learning because of one single story.

It is natural to feel at odds with yourself and your ideals. After all, they are hard to live up to. I started out so certain and sure, only to learn that I couldn't actually fix much. All I could do was try to be as good as I could.

I think once you choose to be a parent, a partner, a friend, there are limits set upon you. To be good at one thing means you have to forsake others. I just try to show up and give love, and to be what someone needs while still saving a little for myself.

Step out of the routine. I know work is important; it feeds your productivity. Habit makes us artists; freedom sustains the artist in us.

I like people who say what they feel. I like art that way too. Art that is direct and says what it feels.

You get up every morning with this day set before you and you have no choice but to be open to what happens. New thoughts and new ideas emerge and you just respond to them. That is a day. You learn, whether you set out to or not.

Not everyone is going to love your work. Not everyone should. It's okay if some people do not even see it when they pass by. Like you, your art cannot be all things to all people.

There is great depth in simplicity. You cannot see infinity, yet it is there.

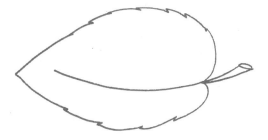

We remain on the brink all of our lives as long as we keep walking towards the edge. The brink can be as safe as anywhere when you are sure of your steps.

Ideas do not have to be complicated to be art. They have to be pure and direct. They have to move someone. They have to be inspired and free. Don't make for others. Make for what is in you.

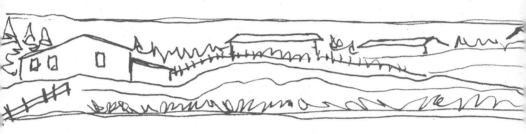

Trying to be better wife, a better mother, a better artist takes up a lot of space in a life.

If I can keep my thoughts kind, my words gentle, my hands creating, and my spirit free as I walk down the road, that will be enough for God, for art, and for me.

Count the stitches or just let them add up unknown, unbidden. It doesn't matter. What matters is your way.

Whether you take a slow quiet path or tread quickly and dangerously is up to you.

Good friends make you feel like you are funnier, and more likeable, than perhaps you are. They listen to you, encourage you, and tell you you are beautiful because they believe you are.

Your spirit is the gift that you bring to the world when you are born. It is the gift you offer your friends and family every day, the gift you offer to your art, and the gift that lingers after you have gone from the world, remaining in the hearts of those whose lives you have influenced.

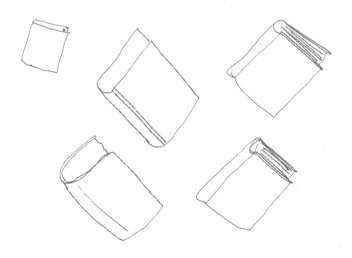

O, Sky, I watch you
    every day from morning 'til night.
I wait for you to change.
    You are such a great example
of how good things
    can be even better.
Sometimes I doubt this,
    fearing that a beautiful life
might see the worst yet.
    Thank you for being above me.
For being a shining example.

The tide was out and there were
huge ditches of purple-brown
mud tinged with white ice, upon a
background of sapphire-blue. I was
    wearing a warm white coat
    and wool socks, the sun was
        beginning to warm the
        day. There was time to
        think.

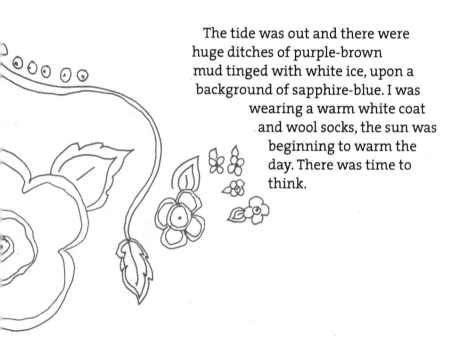

I believe that it is important to wonder about the meaning of art, but I also I believe that a good piece of art should take me to it. It should carry me to the place within myself where it belongs.

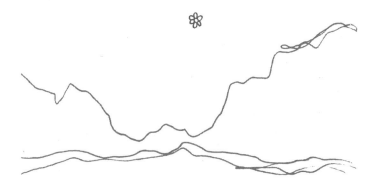

Coming up with ideas isn't difficult for me; they pop in and out of my head all the time. This does not mean I don't work hard, it just means it does not feel like work.

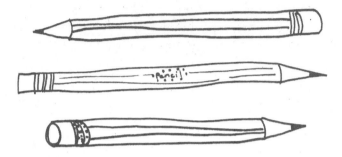

Sometimes I have trouble distinguishing between what is really deep and what is really simple. It seems they are so close that sometimes they are the same. They both go straight at the heart of the matter.

I think the artist's soul, as beautiful as it is, and as appreciative as I am for it, is a demanding one. It needs to be engaged, charmed, soothed, and comforted.

Hands giving and receiving, putting in the time. Learning the motions. Hands on your heart. Hands in prayer. Hands holding wisdom. Hands reaching out to feel the long grass.

Artists absorb the world around them. We take things to heart. We feel deeply. That's why we need to make a private space within us for what's happening in the world—so we can share the burden while still being alone with our thoughts as we make.

A prayer for the man who
fell upon the street.
For the son who walks alone
and lives behind the library.
For the child who cries
when she is away from
home.
For the lonely ones and for the
ones who don't look lonely, for
sometimes they are the loneliest
of all.
For the love that lashes out
when it does not know the
way.
For the tired and the sick and the
ones who weep and for the ones
who pray.

Even something wonderful can take you away
from the thing you truly love.

Light transforms the ordinary into the magical.
Think of how it takes the field in morning and
makes it worthy of a week's work just to capture
it. Watch the light—it is playing tricks for you.

Artists must love the failures too—the ones that
did not quite work out, the ones that did not quite
fit. In these ones there are important lessons.
Lessons that push you forward.

Hope for the fallen.
   Hope for the mighty.
Hope for the makers.
   Hope for the lost.
For we are all
   travelling.
We are all one of these things
   at one time or another.
Hope.
   For us all.

Forget about making art. Just go inside yourself and ask questions. Ask yourself anything. Then make, and try to answer the questions as you do.

You have to believe that the way you do things is the right way and you have to commit to it. You don't have to hate the way other people do things, but you do have to stay focused on and believe in your own way.

I stay close to home most of the time. It is where I want to be. I travel a little, because once in a while I want to. Yet to not step outside a small set of boundaries, to never feel the need, is another kind of amazing.

Dig into your own stories for ideas. Get to know yourself so your work can reflect you. Believe in those small stories, because big stories are really just small stories that have come alive.

Art is made by your spirit as much as it is made by your hands, so make sure you feed your spirit.

There is a sisterhood between colours. Sometimes adding one colour makes me reevaluate every other colour that is to follow. Sometimes the background colour bursts forth as I sit there. One colour begs another to appear.

The real romance with yourself happens when you sit with yourself at the mat and let your mind wander. Hooking alone, letting your thoughts flow freely shows you that making is something you love.

～ deanne fitzpatrick ～

Yes, you are small, but please believe that small matters.

Whenever I start thinking that I must live up to something, that this rug I am working on must be better than the last, I hinder myself. The truth is: I need to forget about what I am doing in order to do it well.

Stay open to opinion as you deepen your work. Trust your own opinion the most, but listen to others whose work you admire. Take it in. Think about it. Grow with it.

A bowl of strawberries on the table.
  Beside them, fresh biscuits.
Summer on the table.
  Mock orange in a jam jar.
Kitchen flowers.
  Humble flowers from the side of the road.
I see it all as I pass through the kitchen.
  It is so fine.

The only place I have learned more than in books
is in the day-to-day of human relationships. There
I have learned how to be good to others.

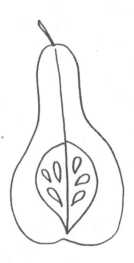

⌒ deanne fitzpatrick ⌒

You have to find yourself interesting. Do things that are interesting. Spend time with interesting people. Read great books, cook wonderful food, learn new things, visit new galleries. Take the time to nurture yourself.

Time is the only thing of value that you have to offer the process. If you want to make really great rugs I think you need to make a lot of them. The more you make, the more you learn from each one.

Use your art to tell the truth about the way you see things. Use it as an expression of yourself, as a way of telling the world what you know to be true and important.

I have sat down at the frame angry and gotten up forgiving. I have learned the truth about myself, both good and bad. I have learned that my hook and frame are my home, I belong with them, and they belong with me.

You can achieve plenty from your own small corner of the country. You can learn lots from there, and you can give lots from there. Your world is as small or as big as you want it to be.

⌒ deanne fitzpatrick ⌒

Sometimes it is difficult to be alone with our thoughts. Sometimes the hooking leaves too much time to think. If we can free ourselves long enough to create a rhythm, hooking will become a meditation and ease our minds.

So sit with it anyway. Try to find the rhythm.

Can you make it as beautiful as you imagined? You can only try. And then try and try again.

Listen to your body. If it says *slow down*, slow down. If it says *rest*, rest. You need a strong body to make art. It not only holds your heart and soul, it is how you give voice to them.

I have to listen to what I hear, see what I see, taste what I taste, smell the scents around me, and touch and feel what I see. That is my job: to pay deep attention, and then to make.

In order to give time to one thing you have to have freedom from another.

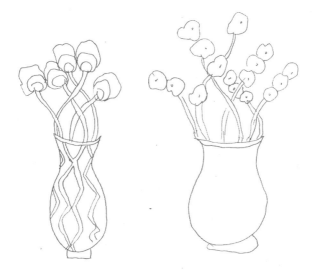

When I get a new idea, I sometimes let it germinate and I sometimes jump on it right away. I don't know that there is a right way to hold an idea. Coddle, plant, or jump on it—the answer is in the moment.

At one time I thought it was important that my rugs be a window into my heart, but as I got older I learned that art is really about what the person looking at it sees and feels.

Sometimes all you need to do for things to work out is to tell people the truth about the help you need. Someone so small in such a little place needs lots of help.

It is in the ordinary things that we find happiness—the rock picked off the beach, the story of a child waiting at the bus stop, the gift of bread from neighbours. I say it is the little things that matter, yet so often it is the big things I am seeking.

Carefully lay that wool on the table and really look at it. Some farmer fed a sheep and sheared the wool and washed it and cleaned it and sent it to market. Someone carded it and spun it and dyed it. All along there was tenderness and love. All along people held it gently. Now it's yours to do with as you will. You are one more part of the story. You get to hold it in your hands and transform it one more time.

There are all kinds of wonderfully foolish reasons to wake up happy.
• The smell of mint in the garden
• Blues singers in bars
• Flannel shirts so big they make you feel small
• Three-year-old cheddar
• Chai with milk and honey
• Bare rosehips against the snow
• Old terra cotta pots
• The happy shrieks of children playing in the distance
• Asparagus sandwiches
• Wool socks
• Handwritten letters in the mailbox
• Little flecks of dust dancing in the sunlight

When you spend four hours a day hooking a rug you have to think about something. Eventually, I suppose, you end up thinking about the way you think.

Today I used the wind to dry a line of dyed wool. The blues are deep denim, to dark indigo, to sandy blue. The last one looks as if red sand will shine up through the water. Sky on sky, blowing on a field of brush and scrub.

⌒ deanne fitzpatrick ⌒

I belong to this Atlantic landscape. It would take years to cultivate a relationship with another landscape that is as intimate as the one I have with blueberry fields, barrens, rocks, pines, spruce, and water. We belong to places, like we belong to our families.

I often stand on my mats just to make the point to myself that this is what they were intended for. No pretense. No nonsense. Just a mat for the floor by the door.

Quiet stitches ease my mind. Counting one, two, three, then back again. I am meandering through the rug like a path in the woods. Counting. Losing count, then finding my way back again.

❀

The inspiration of other artists is a beautiful thing. There will always be influence. But I am careful to never leave pictures of their work around when I am working. I close up the art books. I want my work to be its own.

We were walking down the road and a quince bush was in full coral bloom. Such show-offs, those bushes. The young man beside me said, "That's the thing about bushes; they bloom for such a short time and then they're just green the rest of the time."

I wanted to tell him that this was a metaphor for life, but it was too much to burden him with. I just agreed and walked along quietly.

✿

Close your eyes on your way to sleep and see the images that come forth. Are there dancing girls and sheep in fields? Are there women with their hands in the air? Dragonflies landing on hollyhocks? What do you see when you close your eyes on the way to sleep?

I love the passages in the Bible that tell you not to fear, not to worry. I turn to them time and again for reassurance. That is the story of making. You are alone with your thoughts a lot. You might need some reassurance.

Some summers the apple blossoms don't come on the big tree outside my studio window. I am always surprised, and I wait for a big rush of blooms. There is always hope I tell myself. There is always possibility.

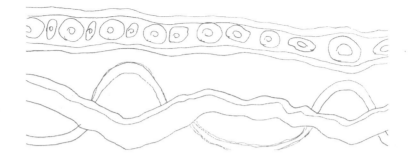

There is always something or someone trying to catch your eye, to draw your attention away. But your own eyes are the artist's eyes. Look where they take you. Follow them instead.

When I hook and I am lost in the motion, it seems I am free from everything. No responsibilities. No pressure. Just me in the moment.

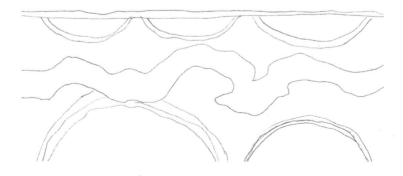

There is no sense in me telling you not to compare yourself to others because you most likely will. I am going to tell you it is okay to do to this for a second or two. Then go to your work and make the work you are here to make.

This week two different friends brought me bags of wool. They brought me the sea, the stars, the sky, the fields, the nighttime, the ground beneath my feet.

On my way down the studio stairs I glanced at my rug—saltfish laid askew on blue-green on my frame—and I got a chill. I was so thrilled with it. It is the greatest feeling when your work gives you a shiver.

When I catch myself going down my imaginary roads of worry, I pull myself back. I say a few prayers. I touch the ground beneath my feet and feel where I really am at this God-given moment. Tomorrow will have its own worries.

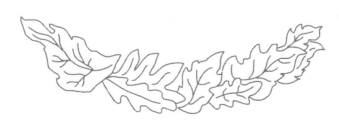

From the top of Amherst on the John Black Road you can see the Bay of Fundy. Late in the day, the sun closes in on it, turning the sky rusty pink. The water shimmers below it. I would have to hook the water all in silk, I think. A crisp blue silk. The rug would be panorama, long and narrow, to show how the bay has scooped out the marsh as if it were just skimming a bit of earth off its top— just taking a little, no harm done.

When I first started selling my rugs, I just set a price. I did not calculate my time or my costs. I just asked myself the question: what can I let this go for? No formula, just a question between me and the rug.

Lost can be a beautiful thing. I like losing myself when I walk, when I make. But it never happens at the beginning.

When I find a new way of doing something I have been doing for years and the new way is better, I always ask myself how I could not have seen it before? The only answer I ever get is that I wasn't ready.

Then there is the doing. The humble doing: the bagging of the jersey, the cutting of the wool. The simple things anyone could do, and yet I do them. Not just for the doing, but also for the freeing.

The maple leaves are shaking in the wind. They are new to summer. They are still perfect. No spots, no holes. Just like I used to be. They are tender right now. Still thin-skinned and waiting for their veins to toughen so they can hang on and be present, even in the bad winds.

Why are painters so much more romantic than rug-hookers, so much easier to love? I cared about this once upon a time, but now I care about getting so lost in a simple project that I don't know or care whether I am celebrated or not.

One of my favorite lines I ever wrote was "My mother's perfume was Javex." When I am near it, it's like she's in the room. And she reminds me that a life is a life, and you must find the best in it and love it however you can.

The other day I was at my pettiest, "crooked as could be," and I found I could not work on my rug because it was so joyful. The happiness of the characters in the rug was too overwhelming. I had to leave it alone for a day until I subsided.

I remember the first time I saw sea-foam green. I was twelve, looking over the deck of the *Ambrose Shea* on my way from Argentia to North Sydney. There we were under a grey sky, with the slick white oily paint of the boat meeting the briny green sea.

I am bearing down on the end of a big rug but I could not stay with it today because my heart and mind were all abuzz with ideas. It is good to relish the last of it anyway. Hang on to the beauty of the finishing.

Even when things are good and sweet and everything you wished and hoped for, there will be difficult moments. There will be times when it seems that retreating would be better than pushing through. That's when we rest, and then we push again.

Making is like that. If you relax and let your hands work loosely, they will gravitate to a natural way of doing things. Your hands will find the best way to carry out the work...if you give them time and freedom.

Wherever people gather, there is tension. It is the human drama. What seems like nothing to me is a high-water mark for someone else. We play off each other like river rocks in a storm, waiting for things to settle so we can find our place.

Walk back to the garden. It is not as you left it yesterday. Never. Nothing is the same twice. The wind is always blowing. The river is always moving. The sun shines differently every day.

You cannot really make art with out telling lies because the way you see it is not always the truth. It is nothing more than your truth, the truth you know and understand, the expression that you are feeding the world. Our work is made with the brush of our own experience.

I am an artist. I am a well. My heart is already broken open. I carry around big feelings with me already and that burden is heavy enough. I stay quiet on many fronts. I need to be able to lift my head and still walk steady down a path.

Don't you just love being with people who know where you grew up? To them, you are not an artist, a nurse, or a doctor. You are not rich or poor. You are what you are, you are what you were, and you are what you will be.

deanne fitzpatrick

The images in my mind will never be the same as the rugs I create. Sometimes the mat is better, sometimes not. Either way, you can't be afraid of the space between your ideas and the reality of your art.

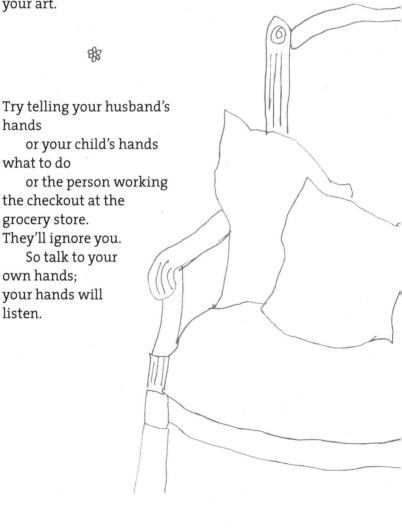

Try telling your husband's
hands
    or your child's hands
what to do
    or the person working
the checkout at the
grocery store.
They'll ignore you.
    So talk to your
own hands;
your hands will
listen.

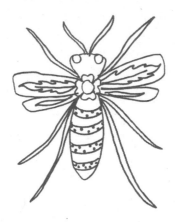

Stop working and make yourself a cup of tea.
Look out the window at the moon. Ponder.
Wonder. You'll never know the answers—that is
the beauty of wonder.

I teach to see the light go on in people's eyes. They
illuminate my own work when I go back to it; I
see it again through their eyes.

August is a month of clear light when everything
looks beautiful to me. What was a field of scrub
in June has become luminescent. On my walk, my
head keeps turning. I am watching the landscape,
trying to remember the light.

I try to leave the work
of other artists to other
artists, especially if I love
it. Then I can only look
at it briefly. I like the
influence to be filtered
through my life, so the
story will be my own.

You have to drink up life—the smell of freshly brewed coffee, the colours of the cliffs, the sound of the birds in the morning, the silky feel of a paper-thin petal of a crimson poppy.

Books are one of my biggest sources of inspiration. They make me think in pictures. I read the words and see images that I might never have seen. They are a window into myself that leads me to want to make.

Today on a walk with Robert he spotted a salamander on the road. The little toasted-orange creature had mauve dots on its back. We took it off the road and onto the grass, because we need to care for the tiniest of things if the biggest of things are going to work out.

An old house is a good reminder of impermanence. This spring there was purple creeping jenny all over the property. It could have been planted two hundred years ago.

One artist asked, "Why would I have black shoes when I could have red ones?" I was telling my husband this and he said, in a sensitive way, "It's almost a little childlike." I said, "Exactly!" Because that is who we need to be the artist: a child, the one who wants the red shoes.

The scariest thing about being an artist is the thought of not getting a new idea. That the ideas will go away. So I make stuff instead of thinking about that.

The impulse to keep
to yourself what you
have learned is a lonely
one. Give freely and
abundantly what you
know and your art will
grow. Because you will want
to move beyond what you
have shared.

Cut short the moments of regret. Meet them with
the courage to move on. Forgiveness for yourself.
Do better. Be better.

The only thing that matters is that we follow
our own vision about the way we want to make.
There are no right ways or wrong ways; there are
many ways. I am interested in the people who
make and how they put themselves into their
work.

For those who struggle with finding what to express: be patient. It takes time. It takes solitude, gathering, writing, reading, and a bit of letting go. You will not always meet your own expectations. Remember that the beginning may not be perfect. There is always the middle and the end.

That tension inside you?
    It is looking for a way out.
It wants out.
    Through your hands.
That's the way.
    Lead it there, out of your brain, out of your muscles, your heart, your body.
    Lead it to your hands.

When I have been wrong, the thrum of the hook tells me so. It forces me to listen, to slow down, to retreat into my home and family, and of course into my interior self.

Handwork is invaluable. It helps us soothe ourselves, and as the world speeds up around us our need to slow down is going to become increasingly important. Pick something up to slow you down.

"Just pick up the phone and call me," my mother-in-law used to say. "You don't have to come over." It is a gift when someone does not put expectations on us. One that often goes unnoticed.

Our stories may not be that unique and interesting. Most storylines have been told and retold. It is your spirit that makes it unique. It is what makes your story your own.

I need to hang on to the girl who thought
barnacles were beautiful. I need to skip, out of the
blue, on my way to getting in my truck.

We all have differing amounts of energy, skill,
talent, and creativity. We are all given the same
amount of time, twenty-four hours a day. The real
gift that each of us has to offer to our making is
the gift of time.

I am constantly trying to convince myself not to get caught up in the get-more, go-farther, build-bigger world. Making helps with that. You can't help but take your time and sort out your truest thoughts while you're at it.

❋

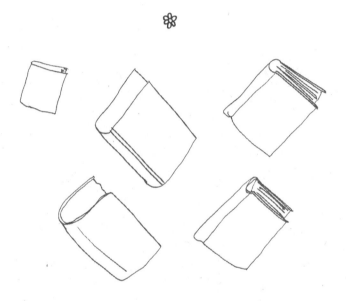

Just because your heart does not break time and time again does not mean you do not carry a heavy burden. We carry our lives, our stories, in that heart. It is the holder of our soul.

I like to think I'm deep but I know I see things pretty simply. I also know that layering simple truths with word after word after word doesn't always deepen them. Sometimes it just makes bullshit.

Time is a funny thing. As we have gotten more and more used to spending money on ourselves, we have gotten less and less used to spending *time* on ourselves. Time can run out at any moment so spend it wisely on the things you love.

I sometimes put distance between myself and others. It is not a distance filled with crisp air; I am still kind. We simply dwell on different sides of the valley. No ill will, just differences. Chasms are part of life. They can even be the clefts of love.

I remember the tenderness of childhood. I remember leaving home, my parents standing outside the bus, and me starting out—not even knowing what an artist is.

Worst of all, or best of all? Can you really ever be sure what it is when it's done? It takes time to know the truth of what you are making. Time away from the highs and the lows of having done it. You need time to know if it is really any good at all.

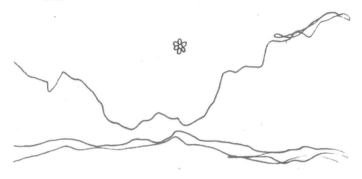

If you want to be an artist, ask yourself what you love to make.

For a while I collected hand-carved crows. I began gathering them as a reminder of my mother, who superstitiously counted crows. But as the collection grew, I found the memory did not deepen. The crows themselves became a distraction. All I ever needed was one.

On Thanksgiving I walked across the top of Canaan Mountain, ankle-deep in blueberry bushes all crimson and frosty. The sun was high, the goldenrod past its prime, but still trying to take back the fields. Partitions of dark spruce. It was a red sea and we walked down the middle of it. I came home full of crimson and dark green. I just wanted to pour it all into a rug.

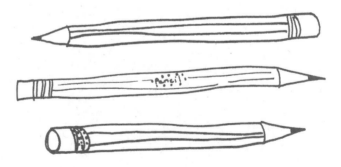

I will use my hands,
    my heart,
my mind,
    to see the beauty in others,
and in the world around me.
    Because beauty matters
and it always will.

I stopped texting my son goodnight. I knew it was
a nuisance to him. He was a grown man with a
home of his own. So I stopped. The freedom of
letting go surprised me; I had been hanging on to
something neither of us needed any longer.

I lie awake some early mornings and wonder. I don't like wondering in the dark, because it turns to worry. So instead I read with a tiny book light because sometimes, some things are better not thought of at all.

I am making a life about the process. It is about all the in-between and all the making. That is where my real work happens. The things I make are just the manifestation of the time spent.

Sometimes I'll hear words fly from my mouth, like a warm knife through butter, saying the things I would usually only think. In the thinking, I realize I am being small, and have no right to judge. In the speaking, I deny myself of my own goodness.

I have faith in God even though sometimes I curse and get mad and think how can anyone be like Jesus? For the love of Jesus. It's just too hard to be kind all the time.

It is not enough to just want to be better. You really have to *be* better to do the Jesus thing.

In a Christmas card, Rachel wrote: "At the holiday, joy is closer, festivity is easier, and change quite possible: the season no longer comes from the calendar, but from us." Couldn't we do this all year long?

My uncle Don would give me fifty dollars whenever he came home. I was sometimes waiting on that money, planning what I would do with it. We do that with generous people—we expect it from them. And it's okay to expect it as long as we still appreciate it.

And in the coming and the going
    I hope I'll find myself
but perhaps I best sit down
    and stay a while
so I'll know her when we meet.

My father always said that keeping your accent
was a sign of intelligence. Sometimes I get quietly
rankled when someone says to me, "Oh, you don't
have much of an accent," when they discover I'm
from Newfoundland. They have no idea of the
storyline in my head.

I've gotten cold shoulders before and been
snubbed, left out.
    So I make to belong. Because belonging is like
being wrapped in a quilt.

My friend Noreen Spence told me she can't stand
people who won't do something for nothing. So
I carry that satchel of words around with me,
remembering that to give freely is what it means
to give.

Take me to the sea
    so I can
        slow
           down
              time
and count the waves of love,
    the waves of grief,
the waves of hope,
    that fill the bay that is my soul.

I am afraid of sending out words to you. I don't want you to laugh at me.

I call a friend who sends outs words and she tells me this:

That it's okay, because as long as you are the you that you are, the words will be okay—maybe even good—and certainly good enough to bring people back to themselves.

For that is why I make.

Why I write.

Not only for myself, but so others will know they are not alone.

I walk and think and thoughts pour out of me onto paper. I hook. Ideas come and go, round and round, and I wait for them to settle down and then I talk to the blank spaces.

Tide washes over everything. The tide of time, the tide of light, the tide of day that turns to night.

Prayer
for the evening
that my heart will be filled
because of some little act of goodness
carried out in the day that has passed
that the sun will set
on the fields around me
but never on my dreams
and that I will rest in the comfort
of knowing my blessings
and in the strength of the knowledge
of the beauty of the things to come.

⌒ deanne fitzpatrick ⌒

acknowledgements

Thank you to my editor at Nimbus, Emily MacKinnon, who helped me shape and form this book into what it is.

Thank you to Mary Williams, who is often my first reader.

Thank you to Angela Jorgensen, manager and a creative director in the studio. We work on so many ideas together.

Thanks to Sheree Fitch for helping me believe that what I have to say is worth saying.

Thanks to Nimbus Publishing for supporting Atlantic Canadian culture and for publishing this book.

Thank you to all the people who support my work and watch the Thursday Lives. You encourage me to create beauty every day.

And thank you to Robert Mansour. He is a good, kind, and patient man who will probably never notice he was included here.